THE SECRET WORLD OF

Butterflies
and Moths

THE SECRET WORLD OF

Butterflies and Moths

Ken Preston-Mafham

RAINTREE
STECK-VAUGHN
RSVP ® **PUBLISHERS**

A Harcourt Company

Austin   New York
www.raintreesteckvaughn.com

Published by Raintree Steck-Vaughn Publishers, an imprint of Steck-Vaughn Company

Acknowledgments
Project Editors: Sean Dolan and Sarah Jameson
Series Consultant: Michael Chinery
Production Manager: Richard Johnson
Illustrated by Stuart Lafford
Designed by Ian Winton

Planned and produced by Discovery Books

Library of Congress Cataloging-in-Publication Data
Preston-Mafham, Ken
Butterflies and Moths / Ken Preston-Mafham.
p. cm. -- (Secret world of--)
Includes bibliographical references (p.).
ISBN 0-7398-4984-0

Printed and bound in the United States

1 2 3 4 5 6 7 8 9 0 LB 05 04 03 02

Contents

CHAPTER 1
What Are Butterflies and Moths?

The smallest butterfly is the pygmy blue from the United States, with a wingspan of only 1/2 – 3/4 inch (13–19 mm).

The biggest butterfly in the United States is the giant swallowtail, with a wingspan of up to 6 inches (150 mm). The biggest butterfly of all is Queen Alexandra's birdwing, from the island of New Guinea in the Pacific Ocean, which can measure over 11 inches (280 mm) from wing tip to wing tip.

With a wingspan of nearly 12 inches (300 mm), the world's biggest moth is the Agrippa moth from South America.

Many tiny moths from the United States and Europe have wingspans of only 1/8 inch (3 mm).

Butterflies and moths are closely related kinds of insects that can be difficult to tell apart. Although small, they are some of the most remarkable and beautiful creatures on earth, undergoing a magical metamorphosis, or change, from wriggling larvae to beautiful and delicate winged adults. They belong to a large group called the *Lepidoptera*, derived from two Greek words meaning *"scale-wing."* This refers to the thousands of tiny scales that form a closely fitting coat on the very colorful wings of most butterflies and many moths. There are about 15,000 different species of butterflies in the world and, amazingly, more than 150,000 species of moths. Someone who collects or studies these insects is called a *lepidopterist*.

THE ADULT BODY
Like all insects, butterflies and moths have six legs. The skeleton of an insect—an exoskeleton—is on the outside of the body, instead of on the inside—an endoskeleton—as in humans. Insect skeletons contain all the soft organs within the outer casing, whereas in humans the soft organs "hang" onto the framework of the inner skeleton. Butterflies and moths have soft exoskeletons

compared with insects such as beetles, and they can be easily damaged if carelessly handled.

Curiously, some moths have "ears" on their bodies that detect the echolocation sounds emitted by bats hunting for a tasty meal.

When it hears the approaching bat, the moth can dive for cover and escape capture.

Butterflies spend a lot of time sipping nectar from flowers. This striking American tiger swallowtail butterfly is feeding on a thistle head, a favorite flower of many butterflies.

Wings
There are four wings (two forewings and two hindwings) that work together in flight.

Forewing

Hindwing

Compound eye
Large eye made up of many tiny hexagonal lenses.

Antennae
Small sense organs for smelling are scattered over the surface of the antennae.

Proboscis
Long, flexible tongue for sucking up nectar and other liquid food.

Abdomen
Segmented tail area that contains the heart, reproductive organs, and most of the digestive system.

Thorax
Middle part of the body, between the head and abdomen.

THE HEAD

The head is small and somewhat rounded. This is where the feeding apparatus, the eyes, and the antennae can be found. The eyes are not like ours. They are composed of thousands of tiny individual lenses that fit neatly together like a complicated mosaic. These "compound" eyes can sense movement very well, which is why it can be so difficult to sneak up on a resting butterfly. However, compound eyes cannot

This is the large white butterfly, commonly found in gardens. You can see the proboscis is coiled up tightly, and the large compound eye composed of many minute lenses or facets.

see detail as well as we can. Moths and butterflies do not have noses. It is their antennae that pick up scents and, in butterflies, also help them balance. The antennae of some male moths are so sensitive that they can smell the scent of a female many miles away.

FLEXIBLE TONGUES

Most adult butterflies and moths do not have jaws and therefore cannot bite or chew their food. Instead, they have a long, flexible feeding tube called a proboscis. This is hollow like a drinking straw and is used like a straw to suck up liquid food. When not being used, the proboscis is coiled up neatly out of the way beneath the head, but it can be unrolled quickly when needed. The proboscis of a sphinx moth from Madagascar is around 12 inches (300 mm) long—several times longer than the moth's own body—enabling it to reach the sweet nectar in the long style of certain orchids. Some adult moths do not have a proboscis at all, but instead have jaws and chew their food (mainly pollen).

Like other sphinx moths (also called hawkmoths), this European hummingbird hawkmoth can hover in front of a flower while its proboscis reaches inside for nectar.

WINGS

Butterflies and moths have two pairs of wings, forewings and hindwings, usually covered in thousands of tiny scales overlapping one another, like the shingles on a roof. These scales are easily brushed off. This is why it is important not to handle butterflies and moths by their wings.

Some butterflies, like the glasswing and clearwing, have wings that are almost transparent, and some moths, like the females of the bagworm and winter moth, have no wings at all.

The wings are reinforced by a network of tiny branching tubes called veins. These help to support the wing as it moves and carries the insect during flight. Flight speeds can reach up to 34 miles (54 km) per hour in some types of hawkmoth, while the monarch butterfly has been known to reach speeds of 23 miles (37 km) per hour.

The wings of this African butterfly have virtually no scales, making them almost transparent. Transparent-winged butterflies are found mainly in the rain forest interior, where they flit around in the deep gloom beneath the trees.

Preparing to Fly

In cold climates, the wing muscles of butterflies and moths must be "warmed up" in order to work properly. Butterflies, like this swallowtail, absorb solar energy by basking in the sunshine with their wings outstretched. Moths, however, are nocturnal (active at night), so they warm up their flying muscles by vibrating their wings very fast for a few minutes before taking off.

BUTTERFLIES AND MOTHS WITH TAILS

Several kinds of butterflies and moths have tails, which stick out from the rear edge of their hindwings. Swallowtail butterflies are the best known for this feature, although not all of them have tails! Swallowtail moths are found in tropical countries and have vivid metallic colors. Some moon moths have very long tails, much longer than any butterfly.

CHAPTER 2
Butterfly or Moth?

It is not always easy to distinguish between a butterfly and a moth. One way is to look at the wings. Usually, a moth will rest with its wings folded flat over its body like a little tent, while a butterfly will hold its wings pressed tightly together and vertical over its back.

This boldly marked hawkmoth has feathery antennae and a plump, furry body. Its wings lie flat out to either side.

 Generally speaking, butterflies are brightly colored and tend to fly during the day.

Sometimes it is only the male butterfly that is an eye-catching color. Bright blue males and brown females are quite a common pairing.

Moths are mostly active at night, and their colors are correspondingly dim. Brilliant colors would draw attention to a moth resting by day and would be invisible in the darkness when it becomes active.

There are exceptions to the general color rule, such as brown- or other earth-colored butterflies and moths that are multicolored and active only in bright sunlight.

Butterflies, like this brimstone, often hold their wings high over their backs, which moths never do. The slender, club-ended antennae and slim abdomen are both typical of butterflies.

However, many butterflies and moths hold their wings out flat at their sides. Fortunately, there are other identifying features, such as the antennae, or long "feelers," on top of the head. A butterfly's antennae look like very thin pencils, with thickened, club-like tips, whereas those of a moth usually resemble hairs or tiny feathers. Moths also tend to have much larger, fatter bodies in relation to their wings and to be more furry than butterflies.

Wing Scales

It is the wing scales that are responsible for the brilliant colors of many butterflies and moths. These colors are produced in two different ways. Either the pigment is contained in the scales like paint (red and yellow are two of the colors produced like this) or the scales are not actually colored at all but have a special shape that breaks up and reflects the light. This results in the bright, flashing metallic blue often seen on butterflies. Below you can see the wing scales of a European swallowtail butterfly close up.

I DIDN'T KNOW THAT

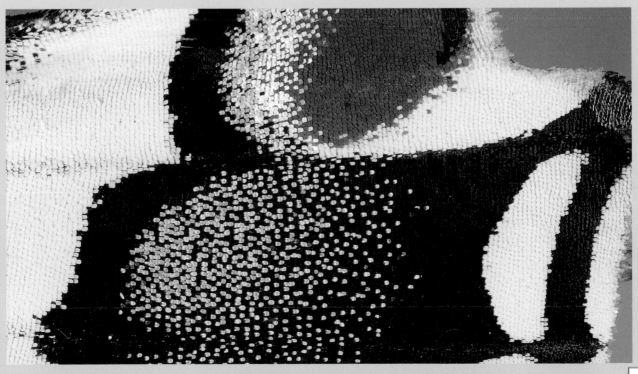

SKIPPERS—BUTTERFLIES OR MOTHS?

Skippers are so named for their darting, bobbing, and vigorous patterns of flight.

This long-tailed skipper is from North America. Like other skippers, it flies along swiftly, close to the ground.

They have always been included in the butterfly family, but in certain respects skippers are more like moths.

They have somewhat fat, hairy bodies and some rest with their wings flat, rather than held up above their back. In fact, skippers share characteristics of both moths and butterflies, showing that the division of these insects into two separate groups is not clear-cut.

BUTTERFLY AND MOTH FAMILIES

Butterflies are usually divided into four families (five, if you include the skippers). Often, it can be easy to tell where any particular butterfly belongs. Most large butterflies with tails are swallowtails. Butterflies that are mainly white or yellow in color belong to the family of whites

A European heath fritillary feeds. Similar fritillaries are found in North America, often on mountain slopes. The undersides of their wings are beautifully marked with silver spots.

This European elephant hawkmoth illustrates how the front and rear pairs of wings beat together. With their rapid blur of wings, hawkmoths are fast and powerful fliers.

and sulphurs. Many of their caterpillars feed on members of the cabbage and mustard family. The brush-footed butterflies are easy to distinguish because they walk on only four of their six legs. The front two are too small to use for walking. This large group includes the fritillaries and browns, as well as the famous monarchs and the mourning cloaks. Coppers and blues are small butterflies, often with bright metallic colors, and belong to a family that also includes the hairstreaks.

There are so many moth families that telling them apart is not easy, especially since many moths are extremely small. The emperor moth family includes some of the largest and most interesting species of all, many of which have large eye spots on their wings. Sphinx or hawkmoths are fat, heavy-bodied moths with a powerful, rapid zooming style of flight. They often hover in front of flowers as they feed, and some can fly backward as easily as forward. At the other end of the size scale, bell moths are rather small, and their caterpillars are often pests. The apple-codling moth caterpillar is an unappetizing surprise if you bite into an apple it has invaded. The small caterpillar of the clothes moth may nibble unsightly holes in your sweaters, before eventually turning into a non-destructive adult.

CHAPTER 3
Where Are They Found?

In some tropical rain forests, more than 100 kinds of butterflies can be easily seen in a single day.

After heavy rain in the normally dry Atacama Desert of Chile, adult butterflies and moths may suddenly emerge after gaps of 10 years or longer.

Some butterflies are amazingly picky about where they live. For example, the Sand Creek variety of the American Great Basin fritillary butterfly is restricted to volcanic areas in Oregon.

In North America, many butterflies and moths of the prairies actually benefit from regular wildfires that keep their habitat from becoming overgrown with trees.

Butterflies and moths are found in most parts of the world. They are absent from the very driest deserts and areas of permanent ice and snow, such as the highest mountain tops and polar ice caps. They live in many different kinds of places, from the bedroom of an urban house to gardens, parks, vacant lots, forests, deserts, grasslands, and mountains.

Along the banks of this South American rain forest stream, you would probably find one or two shade-loving clearwing butterflies. At the edge of a broader river, however, where there is more light, masses of butterflies may be found feeding on riverside flowers, or on salty sand by the water's edge.

RAIN FORESTS

The richest habitats are the tropical rain forests, especially those of the Amazon region of South America.

▲ The rain forests abound in spectacular butterflies. This beautiful green malachite longwing butterfly comes from South America.

There are places in this region where more than 1,500 different kinds of butterflies may be found in an area the size of Central Park in New York City. This is more than are found in the whole of North America, Europe, and Australia added together! Rain forest butterflies, especially the larger kinds like swallowtails, tend to spend most of their time high up in the tops of the trees and are seldom seen near ground level. A few kinds, such as glasswings and others with transparent wings, live on the gloomy forest floor, flitting silently around in the permanent shadows. As night falls in these forests, many hundreds of species of moths may also be seen flying around a light trap set up to attract them.

DESERTS

Deserts are a particularly difficult environment for butterflies and moths, although many of them have adapted specially for life in these dry lands. In the deserts of the southwestern United States, the caterpillars of giant skippers live inside agave and yucca stems. These are tough, thick-leaved plants that are available year-round, even in dry seasons. Some moth caterpillars bore inside succulent, juicy cactus stems, which are also always available. Another tactic of desert species is for the caterpillars to grow very rapidly during the brief period after seasonal rains, when wildflowers are abundant. The pupae (or resting capsules of butterflies and moths) are capable of surviving in a dormant state for many years, until rains trigger the emergence of the adults. When this

A Desert Relationship

Yucca moth caterpillars live inside yucca plant seeds in the American deserts. It is the female moth that ensures there will be a reliable supply of seeds. Before laying her eggs in a yucca flower, she pierces a hole in its base and stuffs it full of pollen. This is the only way in which the yucca flowers can produce seed, thereby providing food for the moth caterpillars and seeds for the plant.

happens, there is plenty of fresh young plant growth for the caterpillars to feed on.

TEMPERATE FORESTS AND GRASSLANDS

In Europe and North America, with their year broken by long, cold winters, butterflies and moths are not as numerous as they are in the tropical rain forests. Temperate forests and grasslands are often not permanent habitats but change over the years. The degree of change depends on various events, such as wildfires, the amount of animal grazing, and interference

Summer meadows in temperate areas such as Europe and North America are often full of wildflowers, which attract butterflies. This painted lady is the world's most widely distributed butterfly and a noted migrant.

by humans. If the grazing of grasslands by animals like cattle or sheep stops, scrubby bushes and eventually woodland will take over and the grassland butterflies and moths will die out.

As a rule, blues and skippers are typical grassland or open country butterflies, while hairstreaks and many fritillaries are often found in wooded habitats.

CHAPTER 4
Courtship and Mating

 Moths, which primarily fly at night, find each other using a special scent. Butterflies, which fly during the day, mainly use sight.

 For some butterflies, female scent is very important. Even a female pupa will attract a crowd of possible butterfly mates.

 Male monarch butterflies chase the females and hijack them in flight, forcing them to the ground, where mating takes place.

 After mating, some male butterflies leave a "plug" in the female so that she cannot mate again.

Individual members of a specific butterfly and moth species are often widely scattered, making it difficult for the males and females to find one another in order to mate.

In some butterfly families, the male stakes out a territory to which the female will come for mating. The territory could be a desert hilltop, as in the case of the black swallowtail and great purple hairstreak, or a sunlit spot in the forest as favored by the European speckled wood. These "landowners" chase away other males, so that when a female finally arrives to mate, she can be sure to

Male green longhorn moths form dancing aerial swarms, which attract females looking for a mate. These males are just beginning to take off for another bout of courtship, having landed on a flower for a rest.

choose him rather than any competitor. Sometimes the females are able to take their pick from a swarm of males, as in many of the tiny day-flying longhorned moths. The males form aerial dancing groups around a tree branch, and the females join the troupe just long enough to choose a mate.

Other male butterflies actively look for females by patrolling along an area where females are likely to be resting. Patrollers tend to be members of very common species, or those that live in crowded conditions in a restricted environment. This greatly increases the chances that a male will come upon a female.

Amazing Antennae

Many male moths, like this African moon moth, have very extravagant comb-like antennae. These are designed to act as "scent-aerials" and can pick up minute amounts of a special sexual scent given off by a faraway female. She may be as far as 6.5 miles (11 km) away, but the male's antennae accurately guide him toward her, following the unbelievably faint traces of her scent wafting on the breeze.

I DIDN'T KNOW THAT

COURTSHIP

Female insects can be quite picky and will not necessarily mate with any male who comes along. In fact, a male may not even be recognized as a possible partner, unless he first takes steps to establish his sex and identity. This means that a period of courtship will often be necessary before the female is in a "mood" to accept her suitor.

In butterfly courtship, the male usually flutters over and around the female. He brushes against her, bombarding her with scent from special scales called androconia, located on the wings. They are easily detached during the male's

Moths mate in a back-to-back position, and may spend many hours sitting motionless on a leaf. This beautiful species is from the rain forests of southeast Asia. Its brilliant colors serve to warn enemies that it tastes nasty.

energetic courtship flutterings and act as tiny "love-bombs," ensuring that the female gets into the mood for mating. In some butterflies the male's scent is emitted from brushlike structures called hair pencils that can protrude from the tip of the abdomen. Some male butterflies give the female a "hug," clasping her scent-sensitive antennae between their wings. This guarantees that the antennae are really drenched in the male's scent.

Many male moths also shower the female with scent during courtship. The scent is derived from scent-brushes on the leg.

MATING

Mating takes place in a back-to-back position, with the male and

Like moths, butterflies also mate facing in opposite directions. Note how these brush-footed butterflies from the South American rain forests stand on only four of their six legs.

female facing in opposite directions. Despite their rather awkward appearance, they are still able to fly like this. In many species the male does all the flying and carries the female dangling beneath him. Mating is usually quite a lengthy process and may take several hours, sometimes lasting overnight. If a female butterfly does not want to mate, she holds the tip of her body upward, out of the male's reach.

CHAPTER 5
Life Cycles

During the lifetime of a giant female moth, she may lay up to 20,000 eggs.

Many butterfly caterpillars, such as the large white, spin a silken girdle, like a little silk lasso, around their middle to support the pupa.

The cocoon of the flannel moth has a trapdoor that snaps open when the adult pushes against it.

Arctic caterpillars may take two years to grow fully, because of the very short summers and low temperatures.

Most adult butterflies and moths probably live for only 2 to 3 weeks.

Like other insects such as beetles, wasps, and flies, butterflies and moths develop through four very different life stages: egg, larva, pupa, and adult.

THE EGG

Female butterflies and moths usually take great care in placing their eggs where their caterpillars will best be able to grow, normally on a foodplant. It is common to see a female butterfly flitting from plant to plant, landing momentarily before moving on. She is making a quick test of a variety of leaves, to

This female emperor moth from South Africa is laying eggs on a plant stem. When first laid the eggs are almost white, but as they age and the caterpillars begin to develop inside, they gradually darken in color.

Ant Protection

Some female butterflies only lay their eggs close to ants that will help protect the caterpillar from enemies. In exchange, the caterpillars secrete nutrient-rich droplets that the ants like to eat. This sort of mutually beneficial relationship is called symbiosis.

find out which one is suitable as food for her caterpillars. She briefly "tastes" each leaf using special chemical detectors on her feet, her antennae, or on the tip of her body.

Most species lay their eggs on the actual foodplant, but others merely drop their eggs randomly as they fly over the grasses on which their caterpillars will later feed. The eggs may be placed alone or in batches. The number of eggs in a batch varies widely. From 10 to about 350 is typical for butterflies, depending upon the species. The eggs themselves are usually shiny, most often white, pale yellow, or green. They are often beautifully shaped, like little colored parcels, with intricate surface patterns and

ribs down the sides. Some moths, such as most tussock moths, protect their eggs beneath masses of hairs detached from their bodies. In others, such as the American tent-caterpillar moth, the egg-batch forms a broad collar around a twig of the foodplant.

Once laid, most eggs are abandoned, but in at least two kinds of tropical butterflies the female stays and guards them. Most eggs hatch within a week or less. Some moths and butterflies, like the white admiral, have only one set of offspring (or brood) per year; others, such as the buckeye, have two or more, and in permanently warm areas some kinds breed all year.

THE LARVAL STAGES

The larvae of butterflies and moths are usually called caterpillars. They may be smooth, hairy, or spiny. Upon hatching from the eggs, the first thing that many caterpillars do is to eat their eggshells, which are extremely nutritious. Caterpillars do not resemble the adults; they are really just long, wiggly eating-machines. Their main aim in life is to devour as much food as possible.

When the caterpillar hatches, its first meal is usually the eggshell. This is full of nutrients, which are too good to waste. This owl butterfly caterpillar from South America will eventually reach a length of more than 4 inches (10 cm).

THE CATERPILLAR BODY

Although some caterpillars appear smooth-skinned, they are in fact covered with many fine bristles or hairs.

Clasper
Used as an anchor.

Spiracles
These allow air in and out of the body.

Prolegs
These stout, unjointed legs are crowned with tiny hooks.

True legs
Three pairs of tiny, jointed legs that correspond to the legs of the adult insect.

THE HEAD

Simple eyes
Small, simple eyes, or ocelli, can detect changes in light intensity.

Maxilla
Guides food into the mouth and contains taste cells.

Palp
Used for touching and tasting food.

Mandible
Has a very sharp cutting surface to chop leaves and other foods.

Spinneret
Produces silk to make the cocoon. The silk glands of some moths are very large.

Since the size of the caterpillar's outer skin can increase only within very narrow limits, it has to be shed, or molted, each time the caterpillar wants to grow larger. Growth therefore happens in stages. The caterpillar quickly expands into its soft new skin, shortly after molting out of the tough old one. Most caterpillars molt five times as they grow up.

Unlike most adult butterflies and moths, caterpillars have powerful jaws and can crunch and tear their food. The head is tough and rounded and lacks the compound eyes of the adult. Instead, there is a group of about six tiny, simple eyes

A colorful cinnabar moth hungrily devours a leaf. The claspers and prolegs cling tightly to the stem.

called ocelli. These eyes cannot make out a picture of the world around them, but can distinguish light from dark. The head also bears a pair of very short antennae that are hardly visible, unlike the long antennae of the adult.

Like the adults, caterpillars have three pairs of jointed legs situated at the front end of the body. In addition, caterpillars have several pairs of rather fleshy and stumpy legs toward the rear of the body. These are called prolegs. Furnished with a crown of tiny hooks, they are very good at hanging tightly onto things.

The time taken for the caterpillar to grow fully is usually 3 to 6 weeks, depending on the species and the temperature of its surroundings.

27

The Pupal Stage

The caterpillar eventually stops feeding and starts to wander around, looking for a suitable place in which to make one last molt into a pupa. In butterflies this pupa is called a chrysalis, meaning "golden," and it may be beautifully spotted with metallic silver or gold flecks. In moths, the pupa is most often a dark, shiny reddish-brown. Pupae may form out of sight in the soil, under a stone, or in a curled leaf of the foodplant, or they may be out in the open on a plant, tree, or rock. Many butterfly pupae hang upside down from a silken

The caterpillar of this South African moth has decorated the silk of its cocoon with a defensive coat of stinging hairs from its own back. To make the cocoon more difficult to see, it has also included a few pieces of leaf, which have died and turned brown.

PUPATION

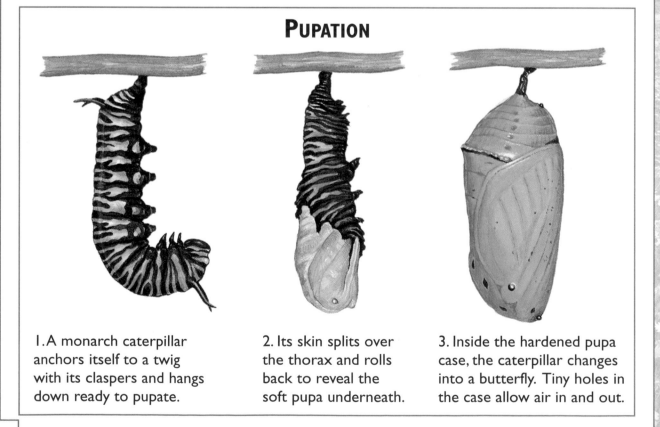

1. A monarch caterpillar anchors itself to a twig with its claspers and hangs down ready to pupate.

2. Its skin splits over the thorax and rolls back to reveal the soft pupa underneath.

3. Inside the hardened pupa case, the caterpillar changes into a butterfly. Tiny holes in the case allow air in and out.

Hanging on the empty husk of its chrysalis, this newly hatched adult comma butterfly has yet to pump up its wings. They are still crumpled after being tightly folded inside the chrysalis.

pad fixed to a plant or rock. Some moth pupae are protected beneath a mass of irritant hairs. Many pupae, especially those of moths, surround themselves with a dense jacket of silk. This is called a cocoon and is spun by the caterpillar before turning into a pupa. All caterpillars can produce this silk from special glands in their mouths. Many species pass the winter in the pupal stage, so the adult does not emerge until the following spring. During this time, it can neither eat nor drink since its mouthparts are sealed over.

It is inside the pupa that the miraculous metamorphosis from wormlike, wingless caterpillar to fully winged adult takes place. Inside the pupa's tough exterior, the larval structures are broken down and replaced by those of the adult. After an average of 10 to 14 days, the adult butterfly or moth breaks free of the pupa. It then pumps blood into its soft, crumpled wings to expand them to full size. After about 15 to 30 minutes, it can take to the air and fly away.

CHAPTER 6
Food and Feeding

Some moths from the American tropics live in the fur of tree sloths; the females lay their eggs on the sloth's dung, on which the caterpillars then feed.

Some moth caterpillars live in spider webs, eating the remains of discarded prey.

The death's-head hawkmoth enters honeybee hives to steal the honey.

Dung left by predators such as lions and leopards can attract a dense throng of feeding butterflies.

▶ This red-headed monster is the large and brightly colored caterpillar of the frangipani hawkmoth of South America. Its powerful jaws can easily munch through leaves and stalks as it clasps on tightly with hook-like true legs.

CATERPILLAR FOOD

The only goal in a caterpillar's life is to feed and survive. Unlike the adult, it does not have to find a mate or lay eggs. In pursuit of this goal, caterpillars are dedicated gluttons, packing away as much food as possible during each feeding session. The majority of caterpillars feed on leaves, using their tough jaws to bite bits off and chew them up. Because leaves are not highly nutritious, large quantities are needed if the caterpillar is to grow rapidly. Some caterpillars eat only flowers or buds, while others eat fungi. Other caterpillars, such as those of the carpenterworm and leopard moth, tunnel in the woody stems of trees and bushes. They often take 3 to 4 years to develop fully, since wood is a very poor quality of food to live on.

When present in large numbers, caterpillars can reduce their foodplant to shreds. This cultivated cabbage is being turned into a skeleton by the many hungry mouths of large white butterfly caterpillars, which always feed in groups.

As well as feeding on plants, caterpillars eat a wide variety of other things. The caterpillars of some blue butterflies eat ant larvae, while others eat aphids or planthopper bugs. The stick-like caterpillars of two kinds of Hawaiian moths catch and eat flies. Many tiny moth caterpillars have strange diets and eat the waxy cells inside honeybee nests, or wool, fur, clothes, carpets, and feathers. Some caterpillars, like those of the California tent moth, feed in such huge numbers on certain trees that they are stripped bare of all their leaves.

Leaf Mining

The caterpillars of many small moths actually live inside the leaves on which they feed. They eat away the green tissues occupying the narrow space between the upper and lower surfaces of the leaf. Their feeding activities create a "leaf mine," visible as a pale-brown blotch or squiggly line on the leaf.

I DIDN'T KNOW THAT

31

ADULT FOOD

Adult butterflies and moths do not usually devote as much time to feeding as their offspring. In fact, some kinds do not feed at all in the adult stage. Since few adults have jaws, most of them can take food only in liquid form. They sip rather than chew their food. Many butterflies and moths feed on the nectar from flowers, probing into them with their proboscis. Nectar is rich in sugars and provides much of the energy needed for flight. Some small moths have chewing mouthparts and therefore can eat the pollen on flowers. Ripe fruits are also attractive to many adult moths and butterflies, especially when they are damaged and leaking an attractive sweet liquid. The sap leaking from damaged tree bark can also be a powerful lure, particularly when it is fermenting and has a strong smell. The fluid oozing from carrion, or dead animal remains, is similarly tasty.

Flower nectar is the favorite food of many adult butterflies. The black proboscis of this monarch is clearly visible as it probes into a zinnia flower to suck up the sugar-rich nectar.

The males of many butterflies and some moths spend long periods of time drinking from the damp, salty ground, since they need the sodium for proper development of sperm. If the ground is dry, they will sometimes squirt liquid out of their proboscis to moisten it. They may also land on the skin of a human who has been sweating profusely and be very persistent and hard to get rid of. Some moths go one step further and regularly feed on the tears coming from the eyes of animals such as elephants,

In many parts of the world, but especially in the tropical regions, it is common to see large groups of male butterflies feeding on salty ground or on animal dung. These striking butterflies are from Africa.

buffalo, cattle, and deer. Harvester butterflies tap into the fluid contained in woolly aphids (soft-bodied insects), but the prize for the most gruesome diet goes to the Asian vampire moth, which pierces the skin of mammals (including humans) with its sharply pointed proboscis to suck their blood.

CHAPTER 7
Enemies and Survival

Like most insects, 98 percent of butterflies and moths do not reach adulthood. Predators, parasites, and diseases, as well as human activities, kill a high proportion of them at every stage in the life cycle. Enemies of moths and butterflies include birds, monkeys, bats, lizards, frogs, praying mantises, assassin bugs, stink bugs, robber flies, hunting wasps, and spiders.

Because of their rather loose-fitting covering of wing scales, butterflies can be difficult to catch. This chameleon has made a direct hit on a butterfly with its sticky tongue, yet has only succeeded in knocking off a few scales, sending the butterfly tumbling off its flower.

The larvae of certain parasitic flies and wasps develop inside the living bodies of many caterpillars. After eating away at the living tissue of the host caterpillar from the inside, the larvae eventually bore their way out through its skin and the caterpillar dies.

Many caterpillars have protective hairs that can give a very painful sting or cause a long-lasting rash.

Even the pupa of the European magpie moth wears warning colors of black and yellow stripes.

Many clearwing moths look just like wasps, with transparent wings, wasp-like antennae, and a black and yellow-striped body pattern. This helps keep enemies away.

Butterflies and moths are part of the general diet of these predators. However, some wasps specialize in capturing caterpillars, which they paralyze with a sting and feed alive to their own larvae. Most adult butterflies and some moths can escape from spider webs because their scales do not stick to the web threads. However, one nocturnal American spider uses a special ladder-like web that knocks the scales off a moth so that it sticks to the silk and can be caught.

Many large moth caterpillars are densely covered in long, stinging spines. These protect them from most enemies and make them very painful to handle. In fact, one caterpillar is so poisonous that its sting can kill a human.

chemical protection against larger animals, such as birds. Any bird eating these caterpillars would become very ill. However, as most of these caterpillars also taste pretty revolting, the birds usually change their minds after a peck.

TOXIC PROTECTION

Birds are among the main enemies of butterflies and moths, and a variety of defensive tactics are employed by the insects in order to avoid being eaten. Many caterpillars feed on poisonous plants and are specially adapted to deal with the toxins. They can actually absorb the poisons into their own bodies and use them as

Many day-flying moths sport warning colors and are easily mistaken for butterflies. This is the scarlet tiger moth from Europe. Tiger moths are found throughout the world and tend to be brightly colored.

colors typical of many day-flying moths, such as the scarlet tiger, and the bright orange coloration of the familiar monarch butterfly are good examples of this.

PROTECTIVE COLORATION AND MIMICRY

In order to try and avoid being attacked in the first place, many caterpillars have evolved a kind of "keep off" advertising sign, usually consisting of brightly colored patterns that predators can easily recognize and remember. These warning colors may be stripes or bands of bold, contrasting colors, such as black and red or black and yellow.

When a caterpillar eventually becomes an adult, the poisons in its body are usually still present. So, not surprisingly, the adult also wears warning colors, although these are often very different from those of the caterpillar. The flashy

Since the warning "uniform" of many adult butterflies and moths is easily recognized by predators, naturally it is beneficial for other species to make use of them as well. Indeed, numerous kinds of foul-tasting but unrelated butterflies and moths all look confusingly similar. This is called a mimicry ring. A few "freeloaders" also take part in these mimicry rings. These take the form of a small number of perfectly wholesome and tasty butterflies that mimic—or copy—the warning patterns and colors of the foul-tasting bunch. Their mimicry protects them from attack. Birds avoid the wholesome mimics on sight, just as if they were the foul-tasting real thing.

Clever Camouflage

Good-tasting butterflies and moths generally try to avoid being spotted by their enemies. Many species are camouflaged, allowing them to blend into bark, leaves, or flowers. Some closely resemble a natural but inedible object in their environment. Many caterpillars, and even some pupae and adult moths, look like twigs, while others are perfect replicas of tattered dead leaves.

A wet, shiny bird dropping may seem an unlikely thing to be copied, yet several kinds of caterpillars do just that, like those of the swallowtail butterfly family. Many adult moths, such as the Chinese character and common carpet, and a few adult butterflies also resemble droppings.

MISLEADING APPEARANCES

As well as copying one another's warning patterns, butterflies and moths—both as caterpillars and adults—mimic a variety of other creatures in order to try to fool or startle a potential enemy.

Many caterpillars, especially of sphinx moths, have eye-like spots behind the head or on the underside of the body. If suddenly touched, the caterpillar hides its real head and brings these spots into prominence. What was originally just a harmless caterpillar now appears to be a large-eyed and dangerous-looking snake! Some moths, like the one-eyed sphinx moth, suddenly open their brownish forewings to reveal a pair of huge staring eye spots on their hindwings. Most birds are rather nervous creatures, so when unexpectedly confronted with this large "face" staring at them, they are sure to take flight.

The "eyes" of this swallowtail butterfly caterpillar are not real, but fake markings that resemble a snake's eyes. The real eyes are very tiny, as in all caterpillars.

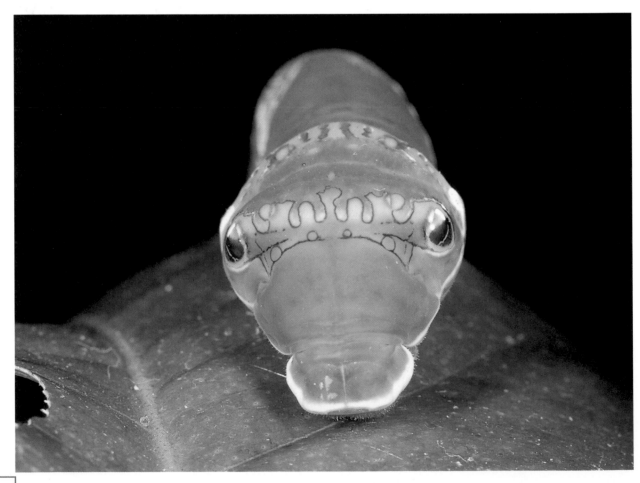

FALSE HEADS

Birds will usually try to take their first lethal peck at their prey's head, having been attracted by the eyes. To take advantage of this, some butterflies—particularly in the blue and hairstreak families— have "false heads" on the tips of their hindwings. These are designed to draw attention away from the real head. If a bird lunges with its beak, it ends up with some scraps of useless wingtip, while the butterfly flutters off in the opposite direction. Some caterpillars also have a false head at the rear end. This is often armored, so that it can withstand a peck, and is marked with eye-like spots.

Many clearwing moths, such as this one from South Africa, look amazingly like wasps. Since wasps have a nasty sting, this harmless moth fools many of its enemies into leaving it alone.

CHAPTER 8
Hibernation and Migration

- Adults of butterflies and moths that hibernate tend to live longer than those that do not.

- Many species hibernate in a state of suspended animation in earlier stages of the life cycle, as eggs, larvae, or pupae.

- Migrating monarchs have been seen flying by tall buildings, like the Empire State Building in New York City, at a height of 1,000 feet (300 m).

- Butterflies can be picked up by storm fronts and carried many, many miles from their migration path several thousand feet high in the air.

HIBERNATION

In cool, temperate lands such as much of the United States and Europe, many different adult moths and butterflies spend the winter in a sleeplike state known as hibernation. They may enter buildings to spend the winter in the shady corner of a room. Caves or hollow trees, or behind dense tangles of ivy, are more natural sleeping quarters. Some moths and butterflies hibernate together in enormous numbers, and each fresh generation gathers together in the same place to do so year after year.

MIGRATION

Many moths and butterflies make remarkably long journeys in vast numbers from one place to another, in order to take advantage of fresh vegetation or to avoid overcrowding in their original homestead. This is known as migration, and occurs mainly in springtime in temperate countries or after rain in deserts.

The most famous and best-studied migrant is the American monarch

These monarch butterflies are in their Mexican wintering grounds, where millions of them festoon the trees. By early spring they have all migrated north.

butterfly. With the coming of spring, millions of monarchs wake up from hibernation and move out northward, laying eggs on their milkweed foodplants as they go. They die after laying their eggs. Some of their offspring get as far as Canada during the summer and make the long migration southward again in the fall.

Escaping the Heat

In hot, dry areas it is the burning summer heat and drought, rather than the cold winter, that create problems for adult butterflies and moths. A few kinds escape the heat by finding a cool spot to spend the summer; this is called estivation. In Australia, brown bogong moths gather in multitudes among the rocky summits of the Snowy Mountains to estivate.

CHAPTER 9
Butterflies, Moths, and People

 Some butterflies and moths live in special nature reserves set up just for them.

 Collectors have paid as much as $1,000 for rare species of butterflies.

 The fashion of releasing monarch butterflies at wedding ceremonies often spreads disease among local butterfly populations.

HABITAT DESTRUCTION

Humans have had a very negative effect on most butterflies and moths. The main problem is the destruction of the habitats in which they live, especially the tropical rain forests that hold the majority of species. The spread of towns and cities has also destroyed much habitat. The widespread use of pesticides has poisoned many species that are normally not harmful to crops. Huge plantations of single crops, such as coffee, tea, potatoes, wheat, rubber, and tobacco, now cover the ground where forests or grassland rich in butterflies and moths once stood.

Collection of some of the rarer species has also been a problem. Very high sums of money are paid for desirable species. Large-scale collecting for display in wall-mounted cases and for making butterfly jewelry still takes place.

Rain forest clearance and destruction and large-scale farming have been responsible for the decline of many butterflies and moths in recent years. Large numbers of species have become extinct before they can even be given a name.

Moths as Benefit and Pest

Moths can both harm and benefit humankind. On the downside, there is the European gypsy moth, which was accidentally released into the wild in North America. It is now a serious pest, destroying huge areas of forest and costing enormous amounts of money to control. On the upside, the silk moth has been cultured for more than 2,000 years in Asia. The huge cocoon spun by the caterpillar yields silk, one of the most prized of all clothing fabrics.

If you want to attract butterflies to your garden, try planting masses of their favorite flowers. This garden in New England is full of daisies and other flowers that are good sources of nectar and attractive to butterflies.

4,000 new species of moths over the last 20 years.

CONSERVATION

Butterflies and moths now enjoy quite a high profile in the conservation movement. Breeding programs have been started in such countries as Malaysia, Thailand, and New Guinea to ensure a supply of some of the rarer species.

Although many species of butterflies and moths disappeared before we even knew they existed, new species are constantly being found. One Brazilian lepidopterist alone has discovered no fewer than

You can do your part toward conserving butterflies and moths by planting a garden containing some of your local native wildflowers. This will provide food for both the caterpillars and adult butterflies.

Glossary

ANDROCONIA – Special scent-scales found on male butterflies

ANTENNAE – Sense organs that protrude from the adult's head

COCOON – The silk covering a caterpillar that spins around itself before turning into a pupa

COMPOUND EYE – Eye with many tiny lenses typical of most adult insects

ECHOLOCATION – locating the size and range of an object (e.g.,an insect in flight) by generating sounds that reflect off the target and are picked up by the ears

ESTIVATION – A hot, dry period spent in a sleeplike state

FOODPLANT – Plant used as food by the larval stage of a butterfly or moth

HIBERNATION – A state of deep sleep in which some animals pass the cold months of winter

LEPIDOPTERA – Biological grouping (known as an order) to which butterflies and moths belong

METAMORPHOSIS – The change that takes place within the pupa to produce an adult insect

MIGRATION – The seasonal movement of animals from one location to another

MIMIC – An animal that imitates another one through similar behavior, coloration, etc.

NOCTURNAL – An animal or insect that is active at night

OCELLI – Tiny, simple eyes not able to distinguish an image

PARASITE – An animal that lives at the expense of another, but does not kill it; many parasites of butterflies and moths should really be called parasitoids, since they eventually kill their host, usually a caterpillar

PESTICIDE – A chemical used to kill insects and other pests on crops

PREDATOR – An animal that hunts other animals for food

PROLEGS – Extra pairs of leg-like outgrowths toward the rear end of a caterpillar

PUPATION – The resting stage following the larval stage (or caterpillar) during which transformation to the adult insect takes place

SKIPPER – A kind of small butterfly, often brown, that has characteristics of both moths and butterflies

SPECIES – A kind or type of animal

STYLE – Part of the female organs of a flower

TERRITORY – An area defended by males, to which females are likely to come for mating

TROPICS – Area of the world immediately north and south of the equator, where there is no true distinction between summer and winter

WARNING COLORATION – Bright colors designed to warn predators not to take a bite

Further Reading

Amosky, Jim. *Crinkleroot's Guide to Knowing Butterflies and Moths.* New York: Simon & Schuster Children's, 1996.

Hamilton, Kersten R. *The Butterfly Book: A Kid's Guide to Attracting, Raising, and Keeping Butterflies.* Santa Fe, NM: John Muir, 1997.

Herberman, Ethan. *The Great Butterfly Hunt: The Mystery of the Migrating Monarchs.* New York: Simon & Schuster Children's, 1990.

Johnson, Sylvia A. *Silkworms.* Minneapolis, MN: Lerner, 1993.

Acknowledgments

Front cover: A. P. Barnes/Natural History Photographic Agency; p.8: London Scientific Films/Oxford Scientific Films; p.9: Ken Preston-Mafham/Premaphotos Wildlife; p.10: Ken Preston-Mafham/Premaphotos Wildlife; p.11: A. P. Barnes/Natural History Photographic Agency; p.13: Kim Taylor/Bruce Coleman Collection; p.14: Daniel Zupanc/Natural History Photographic Agency; p.15: Stephen Dalton/Natural History Photographic Agency; p.16/17: Doug Wechsler/Oxford Scientific Films; p.17 top: Stephen Dalton/Natural History Photographic Agency; p.19: Stephen Dalton/Natural History Photographic Agency; p.20: Stephen Dalton/Natural History Photographic Agency; p.21: Anthony Bannister/Natural History Photographic Agency; p.22: Dr Ivan Polunin/Natural History Photographic Agency; p.23: Jorg & Petra Wegner/Bruce Coleman Collection; p.24: Anthony Bannister/Natural History Photographic Agency; p.26: Kim Taylor/Bruce Coleman Collection; p.28: Ken Preston-Mafham/Premaphotos Wildlife; p.29: Jane Burton/Bruce Coleman Collection; p.30: Ken Preston-Mafham/Premaphotos Wildlife; p.31 top: Hans Reinhard/Bruce Coleman Collection; p.31 bottom: Ken Preston-Mafham/Premaphotos Wildlife; p.32: Jean Preston-Mafham/Premaphotos Wildlife; p.33: Anthony Bannister/Natural History Photographic Agency; p.34/35: Stephen Dalton/Natural History Photographic Agency; p.35 top: Jany Sauvanet/Natural History Photographic Agency; p.36: Ken Preston-Mafham/Premaphotos Wildlife; p.37 top: Natural Selection Inc./Bruce Coleman Collection; p.37 bottom: Ken Preston-Mafham/Premaphotos Wildlife; p.38: Peter Gould/Oxford Scientific Films; p.39: Ken Preston-Mafham/Premaphotos Wildlife; p.40/41: Chris R. Sharp/Oxford Scientific Films; p.41 top: A.N.T./Natural History Photographic Agency; p.42: Pacific Stock/Bruce Coleman Collection; p.43: David Middleton/Natural History Photographic Agency. All background images © Steck-Vaughn Collection (Corbis Royalty Free, Getty Royalty Free, and StockBYTE).

Index

Numbers in *italic* indicate pictures